LONELY PLANET

LONELY PLANET

see it for yourself

Inspirational travel photographs from the
Lonely Planet Images Collection

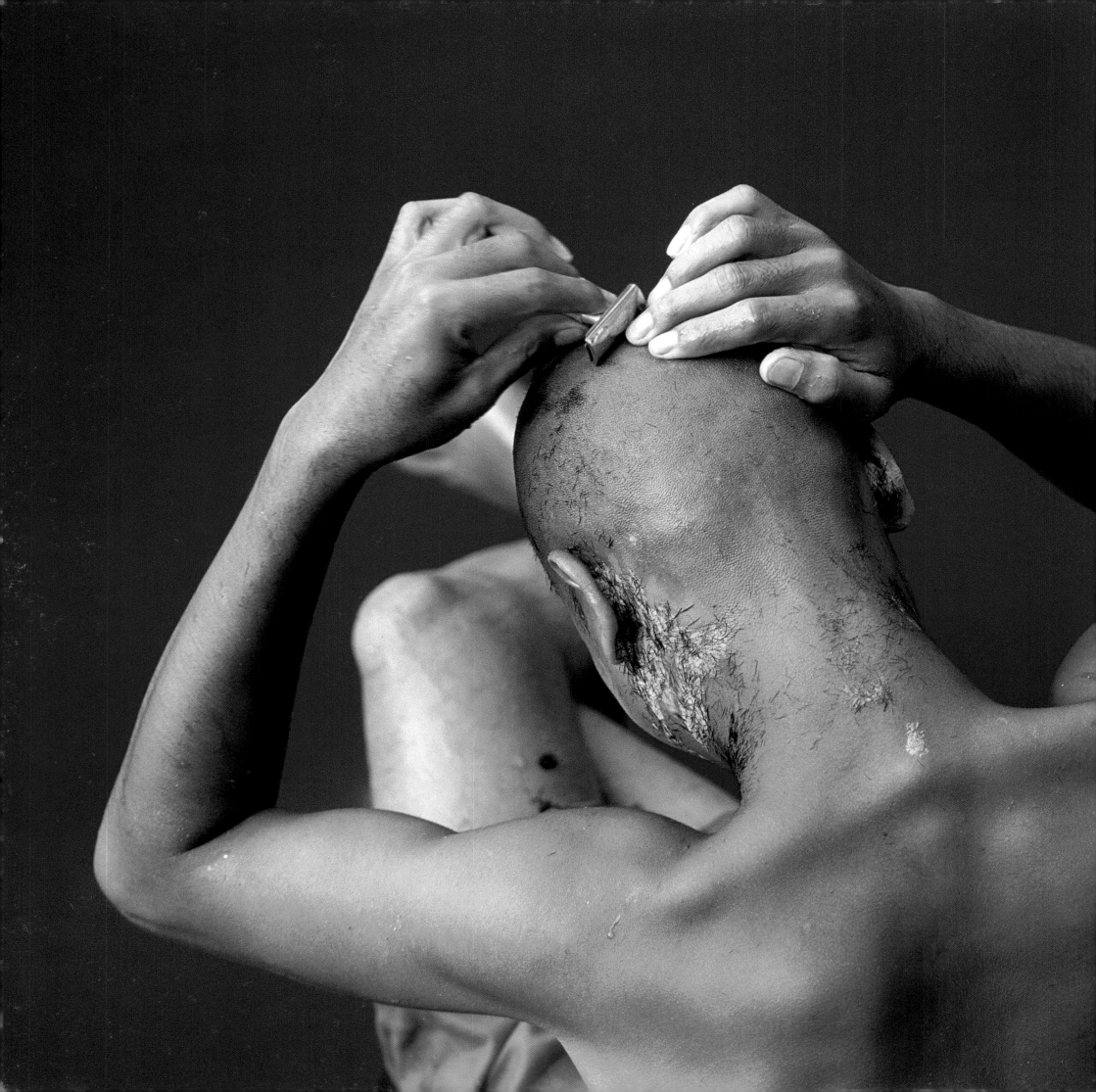

Foreword

It's now more than 30 years since the very first Lonely Planet guidebook appeared on the shelves and, soon after, hit the road in the hands of the very first Lonely Planet travellers.

In the eventful years since the publication of *Across Asia on the Cheap* a great deal has happened in the world of travel. Peoples' horizons have got far wider and destinations that 30 years ago seemed wildly exotic have become mundanely everyday. The numbers of visitors to many destinations have increased equally dramatically, places which once enjoyed a mere trickle of intrepid travellers now welcome them by the jumbo jet load.

For Lonely Planet the changes have been equally amazing. From that first book, which really was put together on a kitchen table, we've progressed to becoming a company with offices around the world, hundreds of staff and sales of millions of books every year. But through all the ups and downs one thing has stayed constant for travellers everywhere, for Lonely Planet and for me: travel remains one of the world's most important activities.

Life on our planet today seems to involve a constant cycle of conflicts, misunderstandings and heartbreaks but travel is an equally constant reminder that we live in a wonderful world and it's a world we all share. Travel is hugely significant for the economies of many nations, it's a source of great enjoyment and interest for enormous numbers of travellers, but even more important it's the most positive way for people to meet people, to realise that we all share the same hopes and aspirations and to prove that we can work for a better world.

Despite many ups and downs, and despite the innumerable wandering roads Lonely Planet has led me down over those years, travel is still, for me, an all-consuming passion. Put a ticket in my hand and point me towards the departure gate and I'm always ready to go. The images in this book are a clear reminder of just why that passion has never died, why my world never seems to get any smaller and why, happily, my addiction is likely to remain an incurable one.

Tony Wheeler – Lonely Planet co-founder

previous page Detail of the traditional costume worn by the people of Ojibwa Nation, photographed in Saskatchewan's Wanuskewin Heritage Park, western Canada.
photographer Jeff Greenberg
number 1

left Ritual shaving, Angkor, Cambodia. Buddhist monks shave their heads to renounce any attachment to physical beauty.
photographer Bernard Napthine
number 2

Introduction

One Planet is a celebration of life, of curiosity and the experience of travel.

The underlying theme uniting the photographs in this book is connection, travel's most rewarding and profound gift, encouraging appreciation of the similarities we share in a world of different cultures, experiences, circumstances and environments.

Chosen from the stunning and inspirational collection of images held in the Lonely Planet Images library, the photographs in this book were selected not only for their beauty and photographic excellence, but also for their sense of capturing a moment in time, a moment that is shared – or at least understood – across the globe.

The photographs capture the essence of *being there*, in that moment. They depict universal expressions of the human spirit shared in very different contexts. Their immediacy is inclusive; their energy, edge and sense of fun invite the viewer into the picture to participate in the shared experiences, emotions and rituals that connect us all as humans.

Lonely Planet's photographers are passionate travellers, artists whose workplace is the road. Their observations reveal the universality of life, sharing the similarities and celebrating the differences. The connection between photographer and subject is often compelling, hinting at the different journeys that resulted in the capturing of that particular moment in time on film.

One Planet pays tribute to the cultural, creative and geographical diversity of the world we inhabit. In particular, the photographs highlight our astonishing human diversity, the divergence and synchronicity that continue to captivate and reward us as humans and travellers. It also celebrates the majesty of the animal kingdom, and the sheer beauty and awesome diversity of our natural world. *One Planet* presents a truly global view that celebrates the many pieces of the puzzle that make up a picture of our surprising world.

In choosing the juxtaposition of images, we have mainly used gut instinct as our guide. The result is that some images make obvious companions – perhaps because they show the same activity happening in totally different parts of the world, such as kids knocking about a football (image numbers *133* and *134*) or people rushing for shelter from a torrential downpour (*119* and *120*). Other comparisons share no connection at all in terms of content, but visually they fit together perfectly. With this artistic licence, then, we have allowed an orang-utan in a rehabilitation centre to sit opposite a Chilean steel mill worker (*147* and *148*), and we have juxtaposed a bungee jumper flying through air with an ice-cutter negotiating a

left The monumental Grande Arche of La Défense dwarfs a class of visiting schoolchildren, Paris, France.
photographer Izzet Keribar
number 3

path through the black waters (*194* and *195*). It is my hope that you, the reader, will see the connections in the pairings we have made, but that you will look with your own eyes, mind and heart to make your own interpretation – in the words of Henry Thoreau, 'the question is not what you look at, but what you see'.

Humanity in all its beauty, strength, weakness, shyness, exhibitionism and spirit is represented here, in the eyes, smiles, hands, gestures, clothing, personalities and situations momentarily captured by the photographers. The two boys who introduce the selection (*4* and *5*) display a shared curiosity, though one is openly inquisitive while the other is far more reserved. A timid Chinese girl is torn between hiding and smiling for the camera in image *83*, while the Nepalese girl opposite her obliges without shyness.

The theme of synchronicity is witnessed in images *10* and *11*, where young kids in New Delhi, India, leap with feverish excitement into ornamental ponds for a cooling midday swim, while in Queensland, Australia, two young brothers in arms delight in the refreshing waters of the Pacific Ocean. In images *140* and *141*, we can see that other young children share the same instinctive impulses, despite one group being in the USA and the other in Indonesia.

Notions of friendship are explored in image *43*, where we see three young Buddhist monks enjoy some quiet time walking together, one travelling behind the other, heading in the same direction. Opposite this photograph are three young men from the Philippines enjoying some spirited time together at the town dump, enjoying each other's company in surroundings that would otherwise appear grim.

Companionship and a certain intimacy are revealed by cultural pursuits. In image *38*, an ear-cleaner on an Indian street serves a customer, while thousands of miles away in Ethiopia, Africa, a man striking an almost identical pose applies tribal markings to his companion's face.

The various physical landscapes we inhabit provide the backdrop to many of the images, and are also individually celebrated as fine examples of nature's drama and beauty. The seemingly endless blue hills of Kathmandu, Nepal, in image *21*, the silky-textured dunes of the Great Sand Dunes National Park in Colorado, USA, in image *56*, and Chile's stunning Andean peaks in image *151* provide eternal inspiration for the traveller. The patterns and colours of Maine's autumnal leaves contrast with the regimented yet striking lines of a British city's rooftops in images *196* and *197*.

Cultural and religious celebrations and festivals enjoyed across the world reveal a shared reverence for tradition, that all-important link with the past which maintains connections with our national and family heritage. The trappings of these traditions are resolutely maintained, in the masks and make-up of the various celebrants in images *15* and *16* and images *68* and *69*.

One Planet also celebrates our shared sense of fun: a film set in Chennai, India (*26*); very different audiences in Italy and India (*61* and *62*); the age-old desire to play peek-a-boo that's common to places as far flung as Nepal and Peru (*92* and *93*). Board games are enjoyed in Hungary and China (*123* and *124*), the outrageous hairdos of punks (*102*) will never go out of fashion, and Sydney's annual Gay & Lesbian Mardi Gras will always attract its fair share of extroverts (*7*).

The juxtaposition of images in *One Planet* is quirky, thought-provoking and compelling. Similar and opposing themes and images are combined, contrasted and compared, while colours, shapes and patterns prove irresistible partners. And of course there's the all-important element of surprise and sheer exhilaration at what has been captured by the photographer. A passing moment immortalised on film, such as the American boy leaping excitedly into the air in front of a graffiti-strewn wall (*116*) or the Nepalese monks viewed as if in multiple dimensions through a doorway (*178*).

In the spirit of Lonely Planet's ethos of getting out there and *just going*, we hope you find these images and words truly inspirational. At Lonely Planet, we are passionate about travel. Through exposure to other cultures, people and places, we can gain an appreciation of the world that exists outside our own window – an appreciation that can stretch over many thousands of miles.

In *One Planet*, the photographers have captured their own small moments that help to construct the bigger picture, where the similarities between us overwhelm our differences. Yet it is only by gaining a true appreciation of both that we can obtain the wisdom and the compassion we need to help shape the future of our One Planet.

Above all, the photographs in this book carry one simple message – 'see it for yourself'. It was through this spirit of adventure and action, through independence and self-determination, that Lonely Planet was born. We hope that the images in this book will inspire you to create your own adventure.

Roz Hopkins – Publisher

An inquisitive novice monk at Drepung Monastery, Tibet. Drepung was once the world's largest monastery, and for a time it was the home of the Dalai Lamas. Today, around 600 monks remain in residence.

photographer Richard I'Anson
number 4

A reserved youngster from Cobquecura, Chile.
photographer Eric L Wheater
number 5

Twin golden girls, Marian and Vivian Brown, hold onto their hats in front of the Bay Bridge,
San Francisco, USA.

photographer Alison Wright

number 6

Matching handbags and glad rags at the Sydney Gay and Lesbian Mardi Gras, Australia.
photographer **Greg Elms**
number **7**

With its vast, crescent-shaped sweep of protected beach, Agadir is Morocco's premier seaside resort,
complete with camels and horses for hire.

photographer Izzet Keribar

number 8

Traversing the Erg Chebbi, a magical landscape of constantly drifting dunes in the Saharan region of Morocco, near Merzouga.

photographer Izzet Keribar

number 9

Irreverently enjoying the ornamental ponds flanking Rajpath (Kingsway), a broad promenade in New Delhi, India.

photographer Patrick Horton

number 10

Brothers in arms enjoy Queensland's fabled coastline, the playground of Australia.
photographer Oliver Strewe
number 11

next page The brilliant blur of a festively dressed crowd at a religious celebration in Rajasthan, India.
photographer Greg Elms
number 12

Whether it's for thrills or fare evasion, train surfing in Brazil is an extremely dangerous activity risked by members of Rio de Janeiro's gangs and subcultural groups. Not only is the train hurtling along at 120 km/h, the overhead cables carry a massive 3300 volts.

photographer John Maier Jr

number 13

Children dressed as leopards and tigers perform at a temple festival in Kochi, southern India.
photographer Eddie Gerald
number 14

Young Mon girls attend to their make-up in the Kanchanaburi region of Thailand.
photographer Bill Wassman
number 15

Masks and masquerades are a beloved tradition continued from medieval times during the pre-Lenten Carnevale in Venice, Italy.
photographer Juliet Coombe
number 16

A well-insulated young shepherd keeps warm in the Simien Mountains, northern Ethiopia.
photographer Frances Linzee Gordon
number 17

An elderly Afghani rugs up against the cold in Shiraz, Iran.
photographer Phil Weymouth

Hundreds of inscribed *torii*, or entrance gates, line the four-kilometre pathway at Fushimi-Inari Taisha, a Shinto shrine south of Kyoto, Japan.

photographer Izzet Keribar

number 19

A marble pavilion at Amber Palace, Jaipur, India. This fort-palace defended the ancient capital, and is a superb example of medieval Rajput architecture with its forbidding external appearance and lavish, romantic interior.

photographer Richard I'Anson

number 20

next page The misty Middle Hills of Nepal are home to the Kathmandu and Pokhara Valleys. Farms blanket the hills in an endless series of terraces planted with wheat, rice and vegetables.

photographer Richard I'Anson

number 21

Robed shadows pass a mosque mural in Edfu, Egypt, site of the famed Temple of Horus.
photographer Izzet Keribar
number 22

Under the shadow of the menorah, an orthodox Jew prays at the Western Wall, also known as the
Wailing Wall, in the Old City of Jerusalem, Israel.

photographer Izzet Keribar

number 23

A cheetah surveys his surroundings from the vantage point of a termite mound on the plains of Namibia.

photographer Dave Hamman

number 24

A lava lizard pauses beneath a full moon in the Galápagos Islands, Ecuador.
photographer Mark Newman
number 25

next page *Jaws* Indian style at Film City Studios in Chennai (Madras), India. Chennai's prolific film
industry now rivals that of Mumbai's Bollywood.
photographer Eddie Gerald
number 26

The Kikuyu, Kenya's largest tribal group, place immense social importance on the role of the witch doctor, whose lofty position is reflected in the size of his headdress.

photographer David Wall

number 27

All made up, a dancer prepares to perform Kathakali, a classical art form of dance and theatre from Kerala on India's southern tip. Traditionally lasting several hours, the performances are based on Indian epics such as the *Ramayana* and the *Mahabharata*.

photographer Eddie Gerald

number 28

Perhaps travel cannot prevent bigotry, but by demonstrating that all peoples cry, laugh, eat, worry, and die, it can introduce the idea that if we try and understand each other, we may even become friends.

- Maya Angelou

Filtered sunlight patterns a gaudily painted house on the island of Santorini (Thira)
in the Cyclades, Greece.
photographer Izzet Keribar
number 30

Lantern shadows on a wall of the Heian-jingu, a bright orange Shinto shrine designed as a replica of the ancient imperial palace in Kyoto, Japan.
photographer Frank Carter
number 31

next page Evening draws in for local boys beneath the streetlights of Madang, Papua New Guinea.
photographer Jerry Galea
number 32

Mao Zedong keeps a watchful eye over the Gate of Heavenly Peace, Tiananmen, Beijing. For centuries the gate has been the official entrance to the Imperial Palace, the heart of power in dynastic China.

photographer Phil Weymouth

number 33

'Double 10th Day' in Taipei: Taiwan's National Day, on 10 October, celebrates the overthrow of dynastic rule in China led by Dr Sun Yat-sen with fireworks displays and military parades.
photographer **Alain Evrard**
number **34**

A fisherman casts his drift net in the turquoise shallows of Phuket's Patong beach, Thailand.
photographer Tom Cockrem
number 35

A nomad from the remote Chang Tang – the world's highest plateau, in northern Tibet –
demonstrates her skill with a sling.
photographer **Bill Wassman**
number **36**

The Karo tribe of Ethiopia are known for their elaborate body painting, using chalk and crushed ore to imitate the spotted plumage of the guinea fowl. These two warriors are from the village of Kolcho in the Omo National Park.

photographer Ariadne Van Zandbergen

number 37

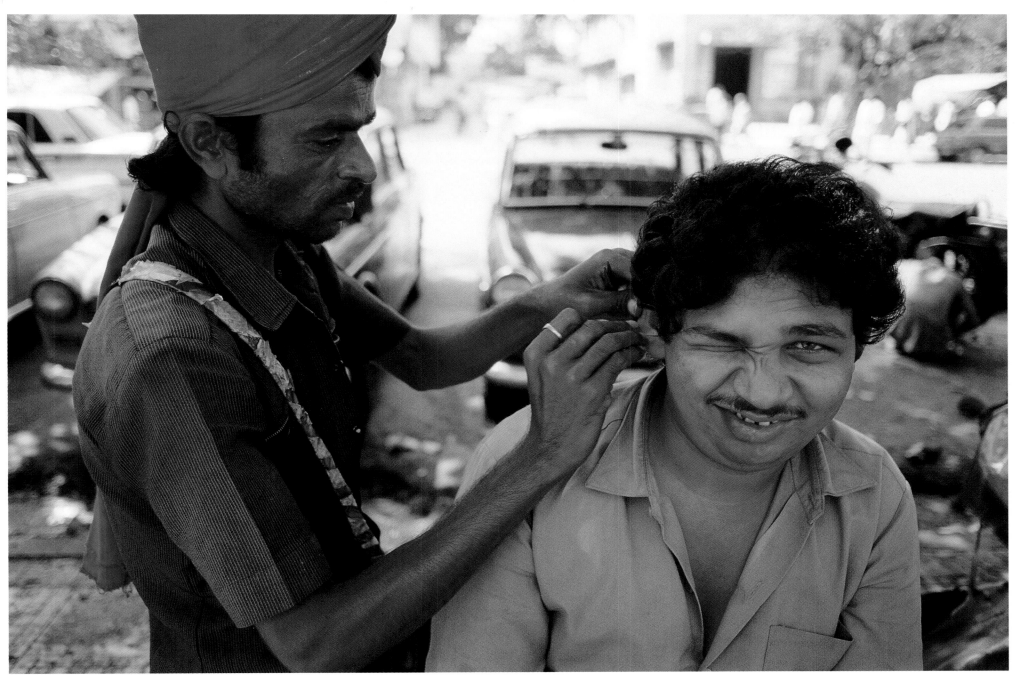

An ear cleaner at work on a busy Mumbai street, India.
photographer Greg Elms
number 38

next page A young woman peeks through the shutters to catch a glimpse of life behind the brightly patterned facade of this Spanish home on the Costa del Sol, Andalusia.
photographer Bill Wassman
number 39

A lone figure hikes across the gentle curves of the Algodones Dunes in the Imperial Sand Dunes Recreations Area, California, USA.
photographer **Mark Newman**
number **40**

Among the glaciated mountains of Alaska's Chugach National Forest, USA, waterfalls freeze, forming vertical walls perfect for ice climbing.
photographer Mark Newman
number 41

This town dump in Quezon City, Philippines, is not only a playground for these kids, but also their home.
In July 2000 many residents of a Quezon dump were killed when the site collapsed following heavy rains.
photographer Richard I'Anson
number 42

Buddhist monks in their bright saffron robes walk through a lily pond in the village of Bavel, Cambodia.
photographer Jerry Galea
number 43

A Chilean boy presents his chicken for the camera.
photographer Eric L Wheater
number 44

Carrying chickens by their feet, Santo Domingo de los Colorados, Ecuador.
photographer Eric L Wheater
number 45

The bronze *Bronco Buster*, depicting a wild-horse tamer and created by Alexander Proctor in 1920, is one of many statues in City Park in the heart of Denver, USA, which celebrate the area's past.

photographer Lee Foster

number 46

Practice makes perfect: a 44-gallon drum provides the perfect fill-in for a bucking bronco as members of the Juwulinypany Community rehearse their moves in readiness for an upcoming rodeo in the Kimberley, Australia.

photographer Richard l'Anson

number 47

next page Three women catch up for a chat after the weekly market in Chichicastenango, Guatemala. Villagers travel from miles around to trade at the famous market, which has been held in this isolated town since long before the Spanish conquest.

photographer Jeffrey N Becom

number 48

Worshippers in their Sunday best at the Paofai Protestant Church of Pape'ete, Tahiti.
photographer Jean-Bernard Carillet
number **49**

The traditional dress of the Dai people includes a protective bamboo hat, worn here for temple celebrations in Ruili, southern China.
photographer Bradley Mayhew
number 50

The question is not what you look at, but what you see.
- *Henry David Thoreau*

left A young bride wears the traditional beaded necklaces of the Karo people, Ethiopia.
photographer Frances Linzee Gordon
number 51

Camel herders make camp in the Great Thar Desert of Rajasthan, India.
photographer Dallas Stribley
number 52

A camel ride operator waits on his decorated camel by the Great Pyramid of Khufu (also known as Cheops) at Giza, Egypt. The pyramid was built over a 20-year period ending in 2570 BC.

photographer Jeff Greenberg

number 53

A picture of concentration: an elderly priest studies the Holy Scriptures in Lalibela, Ethiopia.
photographer Frances Linzee Gordon
number 54

Monks at morning prayers in the sermon hall at Wat Pho, Bangkok, Thailand.
photographer Richard I'Anson
number 55

next page The endless dunes of the Great Sand Dunes National Park in Colorado, USA, are like something from the realms of fantasy.
photographer Karl Lehmann
number 56

Revellers in Kano, Nigeria, enjoying the durbar, or cavalry procession, in the four-day festival celebrated
for the two Islamic holidays at the end of Ramadan and at Tabaski, 69 days later.
photographer Jane Sweeney
number 57

Well-known for their physical beauty, eligible Wodaabé bachelors line up to be selected by single women during the Cure Salée (Salt Festival), Agadez, Niger.

photographer Antony V Giblin

number 58

A local man takes a breather among the unforgiving, dramatic hills of Italy's isolated southern region of Basilicata.
photographer Bill Wassman
number 59

An agricultural worker from Galicia in northwest Spain takes a well-earned break.
photographer **Bill Wassman**
number **60**

Animated spectators in the normally sleepy town of Viareggio in Italy's Tuscany region look on at Carnevale, three weeks of floats, fireworks and fun.

photographer Dallas Stribley

number 61

Pilgrims at the Maha Kumbh Mela, the largest religious festival in the world, make an offering at the holy confluence of the Ganges and Yamuna Rivers in Allahabad, India.

photographer Richard I'Anson

number 62

The therapeutic qualities of volcanic mud are put to the test in Sicily, Italy.
photographer Dallas Stribley
number 63

A naked *sadhu*, or wandering Hindu holy man who has given up the worldly life, encamped at the Maha Kumbh Mela, the largest and holiest fair in India, held every 12 years at Allahabad.
photographer Richard l'Anson
number 64

Lazy late afternoon shadows in the Peloponnesian town of Nafplio, Greece.
photographer Glenn Beanland
number 65

Ships of the desert cross the vast and drifting sea of sand dunes of
Erg Chebbi near Merzouga, Morocco.
photographer Kristin Piljay
number 66

next page A group of colourfully clad dancers perform *capoeira*, a fluid Brazilian martial art with music
and singing, on the streets of Salvador da Bahia, Brazil.
photographer John Maier Jr
number 67

A New Zealand Maori dancer proudly shows his contemporary and indigenous tribal *mokos* (tattoos).
Traditional Maori tattooing, which never completely died out, is experiencing a renaissance in recent years.
photographer Phil Weymouth

number 68

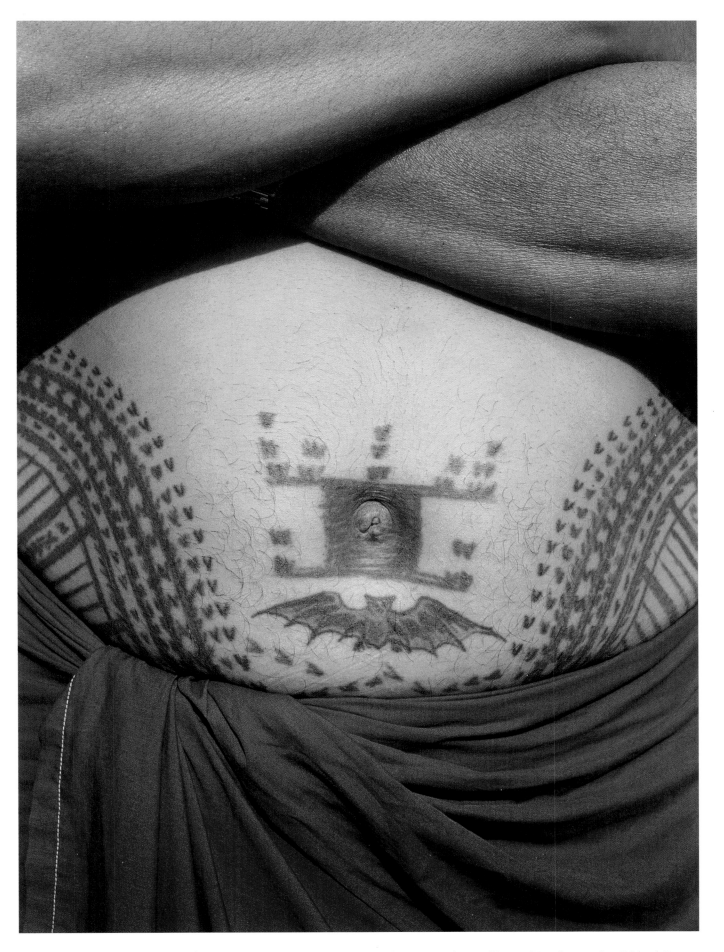

Standing proud, a Samoan shows off his traditional tattoo, Savai'i Island, Samoa.

photographer Peter Hendrie

number 69

Catching a commuter train in San Jose, USA.
photographer Ray Laskowitz
number 70

Seeing life from a tram in Lisbon, Portugal – the best way to get around town.
photographer Christopher Groenhout
number 71

next page A school of anthias flits over brain coral on the sea floor of Ras Mohammed National Park in Egypt. The marine park is often referred to as the 'jewel of the Red Sea'.
photographer Mark Webster
number 72

A young boy collects water from a stream in the Himalayan Langtang Valley, Nepal.
photographer Richard l'Anson
number 73

After a long day's fishing, a cormorant and his master settle on the banks of the River Li in Yangshuo, China, backed by the famed limestone pinnacles of Guangxi province. A trained cormorant is a valuable commodity in China, delivering rather than swallowing the fish it catches because of the ring encircling its throat.

photographer Diana Mayfield

number 74

There are only two ways to live your life. One is as though nothing is a miracle.
The other is as though everything is a miracle.
- *Albert Einstein*

This traditional diver is a member of the nomadic Bajau people, or 'Sea Gypsies', from the Togean Islands of Sulawesi, Indonesia. The Bajau's few concessions to modernity include handmade goggles fashioned from wood and glass.

photographer Greg Elms

number 76

A boy stands guard over a clutch of dugout canoes carved from hollowed logs in Beni, Bolivia.
photographer Eric L Wheater
number 77

The eye-catching colours of *tika* powders are a common sight in Indian markets, such as this one in Chidambaram, Tamil Nadu. Devout Hindus mark their foreheads with the colourful powder, drawing attention to the body's spiritual nerve centre.

photographer Eddie Gerald

number 78

Essential for the Latin rhythms of the merengue, *tambores* await their
moment in Santo Domingo, Dominican Republic.
photographer Alfredo Maiquez
number 79

next page Slender minarets and bulbous domes rise out of the fog over Eyüp, one of the most religious
areas of Istanbul, Turkey. The suburb's Sultan Camii Mosque is a sacred Islamic site,
ranking after Mecca, Medina and Jerusalem.
photographer Izzet Keribar
number 80

A city reflected and refracted, from the Adelphi Hotel, Melbourne, Australia.
photographer John Hay
number 81

The razzle and dazzle of the annual Sydney Gay and Lesbian Mardi Gras, a celebration for gay Australians since 1978.
photographer Greg Elms
number 82

This traditionally dressed Miao girl wears a headdress woven from the hair of her relatives and ancestors. The Miao (Hmong) people are one of China's 55 officially recognised ethnic minorities.
photographer Keren Su
number 83

A girl carrying her brother lingers in one of the intricately carved doorways that contribute to the distinctive medieval atmosphere of Bhaktapur, Nepal.

photographer **Alison Wright**

number **84**

Children on the confetti-strewn streets of Viareggio, Italy, enjoy the extravagances of the town's three-week Carnevale before the abstinence of Lent.

photographer Dallas Stribley

number 85

Surrounded by scattered flowers, a *sadhu* displays his sword, Kathmandu, Nepal. A *sadhu* is a Hindu holy man who has forsaken family connections and material possessions for a life of spiritual devotion.

photographer **Bill Wassman**

number 86

Young women of the Lisu hill tribe, a people known for their friendly and outspoken nature,
at their home near Chiang Dao, Thailand.
photographer Jerry Alexander
number 87

Residents of Elizabeth in New Jersey, USA, watch the world go by from their front fences.
photographer Ionas Kaltenbach
number 88

next page Tharu children playing with paper windmills. The Tharu people inhabit the flat fertile lands
of the Terai region in western Nepal.
photographer Gareth McCormack
number 89

Taking tea at the Paljorling Tibetan Refugee Settlement, Pokhara, Nepal.
photographer Alison Wright

number 90

An elderly woman in Lisbon, Portugal, wears the traditional sombre dress that reflects her gender and age.

photographer Bill Wassman

number 91

The enlightened and the inquisitive at Tengboche Monastery during the annual Mani Rimdu Festival
of dance and music, Sagarmatha, Nepal.
photographer Richard I'Anson
number 92

A woman peers from between the brilliant costumes of dancers at Inti Raymi, or the Festival of the Sun, near Cuzco, Peru. The winter solstice festival which ensured the return of spring was one of the most important rituals of the ancient Incas; today performances and festivities take place at the archaeological complex of Sacsayhuamán.
photographer Richard I'Anson
number 93

next page Twenty-five thousand of the faithful can fit into the courtyard of the Jama Masjid in Old Delhi, India. The largest mosque in the country, it is used for worship on Friday, Islam's holy day.
photographer Chris Mellor
number 94

In the small Moroccan town of Sidi Slimane, locals wait for the train south to Casablanca or Marrakesh.
photographer Simon Bracken
number 95

Elephants congregate at a waterhole in the Addo Elephant National Park, a reserve protecting the remnants of the great herds that once roamed South Africa's Eastern Cape.

photographer Richard I'Anson

number 96

The poetry of motion. The real way to travel. The only way to travel. Here today –
next week, tomorrow! Villages skipped, towns and cities jumped – always somebody else's horizon!
- Toad from Kenneth Grahame's Wind in the Willows

left Street parades, bright costumes, live music, food, fashion and frivolity cram the streets of west
London, England, for the annual Notting Hill Carnival.
photographer David Wall
number 97

Buttons decorate the hair of a Tajik woman holding her child in the Pamir Plateau region of
Xinjiang, China.
photographer Keren Su
number 98

A child from the Koho hill tribe cradles a baby at Chicken Village (named for its huge statue of a chicken), Lam Dong, Vietnam.

photographer John Banagan

number 99

Horses attempt to give a bogged Zhiguli a tow out of the snow and mud at Lake Song-Kol, Kyrgyzstan.
photographer Bradley Mayhew
number 100

The trendy Art Deco district of South Beach in Miami, USA, is a spectacle of bright architectural facades and vintage roadsters.

photographer Jon Davison

number 101

A distinctive hairstyle spotted at the annual Pride March in Melbourne, Australia. The march is part of the Midsumma Festival, highlight of the local lesbian and gay calendar and showcasing a wide range of theatrical, musical, artistic and sporting events.

photographer Krzysztof Dydynski

number 102

Liberty Enlightening the World, the best-known landmark of New York City, USA. It is said that the seven rays of Lady Liberty's crown represent the seven seas and seven continents.
photographer Mark Newman
number 103

next page Afternoon sun illuminates the striking red rock formations of Monument Valley, Utah, USA.
photographer Rob Blakers
number 104

Fashion and glamour on the field are as much a part of the Spring Racing Carnival as the horse races in Melbourne, Australia.
photographer James Braund
number 105

The Glastonbury Festival, a three-day extravaganza of music and mayhem in Somerset, England, attracts all sorts.

photographer Guy Moberly

number 106

A young woman of the Mursi people from the Lower Omo Valley, Ethiopia. The clay or wood plates inserted in the lower lips of Mursi women are a mark of beauty and social status, indicating how many cattle will be demanded for the woman's dowry.

photographer Frances Linzee Gordon

number 107

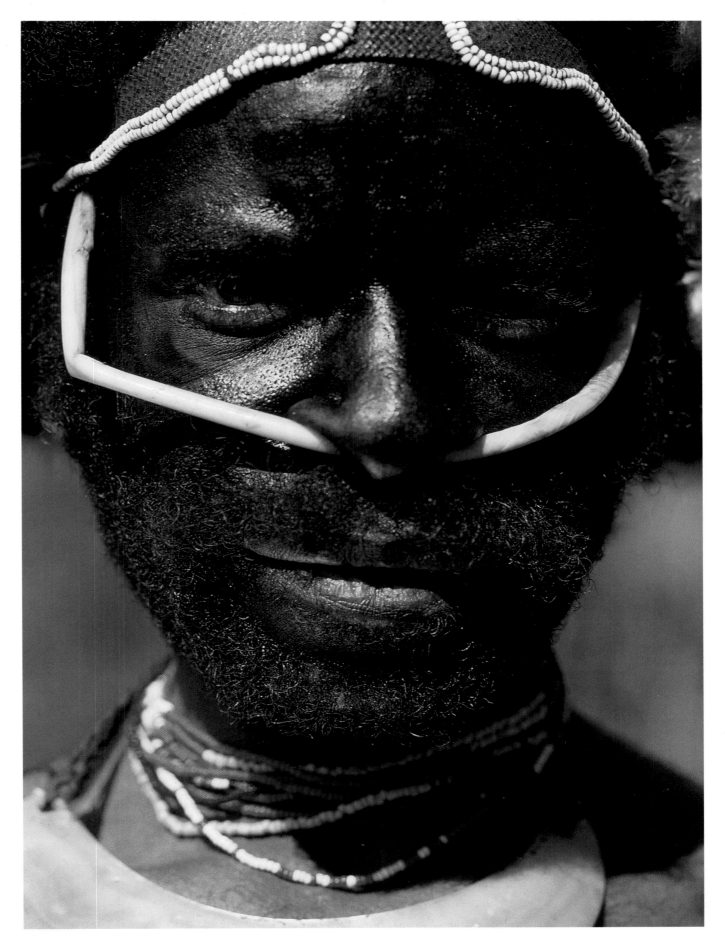

The ceremonial dress of the Central Highlands, East Sepik, Papua New Guinea.

photographer Jonathan Chester

number 108

Once described as the 'flags of nations' by the city's mayor, strings of laundry hanging above the maze of narrow streets used to be a common sight throughout Shanghai, China, until an environmental law banned the practice in major streets and tourist areas.

photographer Keren Su

number 109

The Hills Hoist clothesline has become an Australian icon, representing Australian ingenuity and invention. It's now been around for over 50 years and is as much at home in cosmopolitan Sydney as it is in back yards such as this one on the Cape York Peninsula, Queensland.

photographer Oliver Strewe

number 110

Twenty years from now you will be more disappointed by the things you didn't do than by the ones you did do. So throw off the bowlines. Sail away from the safe harbor. Catch the trade winds in your sails. Explore. Dream. Discover.

- Mark Twain

left A colourfully dressed girl from Rajasthan, northern India, an area known for its folk-art jewellery, textiles and embroidery.
photographer John Hay
number 111

Three lonely emperor penguins on the frozen Weddell Sea, Antarctica.
photographer David Tipling
number 112

A creche of emperor penguin chicks and their adult guardians hunker down as freezing winds sweep over the Weddell Sea, Antarctica.

photographer David Tipling

number 113

Swirls of incense sticks are spread out in the sun to dry in Luang Prabang, Laos.
photographer Bernard Napthine
number 114

The pungent smoke of burning joss sticks obscures the exquisite woodcarvings of Phuoc Hai Tu (Jade Emperor Pagoda), one of the most spectacularly colourful pagodas in Ho Chi Minh City, Vietnam.

photographer Alain Evrard

number 115

next page Practising karate kicks in the schoolyard in New York City, USA.

photographer Eric L Wheater

number 116

The lion's mane headdress is a Masai warrior's most prized possession as it proclaims he has killed a lion in a successful hunt.
photographer Anders Blomqvist
number 117

A Khmer monk experiences the wonder of a solar eclipse at Angkor Wat, Cambodia.

photographer **Mick Elmore**

number **118**

The bus station, Kodaikanal, India. The road to the mountain town is sometimes washed away during particularly heavy monsoon rains, leaving the inhabitants isolated.
photographer Sara-Jane Cleland
number 119

Force eight typhoon winds hit pedestrians on the streets of Hong Kong, China.
photographer Phil Weymouth
number 120

An Indian man on Ahalya Bai's Ghat in Varanasi, India. The ghat is one of the riverside platforms lining the Ganges that form the focal point of Varanasi's most intimate rituals of life and death.
photographer Richard I'Anson
number 121

A San woman enjoys a home-made pipe in Sesfontein, Namibia. The country's few remaining San people are descended from Southern Africa's earliest inhabitants.

photographer Mitch Reardon

number 122

A popular pastime: gathering for games of chess while taking the waters at the naturally heated Széchenyi Bath, Budapest, Hungary.
photographer David Greedy
number 123

An intense game of checkers is played out in Beijing's Tiantan Park, China. The park is a popular meeting place and venue for outdoor games and t'ai chi.

photographer Glenn Beanland

number 124

A journey of a thousand miles starts in front of your feet.

- Lao-tzu

left With the event about to begin, a sumo wrestler completes a last-minute stretch in Nagoya, Japan.
photographer Richard I'Anson
number 125

A group of young males from a traditional village on Tanna Island, Vanuatu, perform one of the many intricate dances that enact legends and play a role in unifying the villages.

photographer Peter Hendrie

number 126

A blur of shoppers at Nanjing Lu, Shanghai's glitzy, neon-lit, pedestrian-only shopping strip, China.
photographer Ray Laskowitz
number 127

next page A speciality of North Korea is the Mass Games, where thousands of people perform
military-style parades and mass-gymnastics displays in perfect and spectacular unison.
The women in blue represent winter in these Arirang games in Pyongyang.
photographer Tony Wheeler
number 128

Chiles (chillies), that staple of Mexican cuisine, for sale in New Mexico, USA.

photographer Ray Laskowitz

number 129

Sorting dried red chillies outside Yangon, Myanmar (Burma). Chillies are a popular means of spicing up the staple diet of rice and noodles.

photographer Juliet Coombe

number 130

The valleys of South-West National Park in Tasmania, Australia, shrouded in tranquil dawn mist.

photographer Grant Dixon

number 131

A storm rages at Patriot Hills in the Ellsworth Mountains, Antarctica.
photographer **David Tipling**
number **132**

Boys play football on the pastel-painted streets of Puerto Limón, Costa Rica.
photographer Eric L Wheater
number 133

Children play in the lagoon of Funafuti Atoll in the tiny island nation of Tuvalu.
photographer Peter Bennetts

number 134

A colossal *moai* statue at the restored Ahu Tongariki site on Easter Island (Rapa Nui), Chile. How the island's ancient people managed to sculpt hundreds of these statues from hard volcanic basalt and transport them from inland quarries to the coast remains a mystery.

photographer Brent Winebrenner

number 135

A fisherman from the southern Aegean island of Mykonos, Greece, wears the traditional cap associated with his trade as he savours an early-morning cigarette.

photographer Jerry Galea

number 136

next page A bloat of hippopotamuses jostle for space in Katavi National Park, western Tanzania. The river is reduced to a trickle in the dry season.

photographer Ariadne Van Zandbergen

number 137

Smiling for the camera, Niger.
photographer Oliver Strewe
number 138

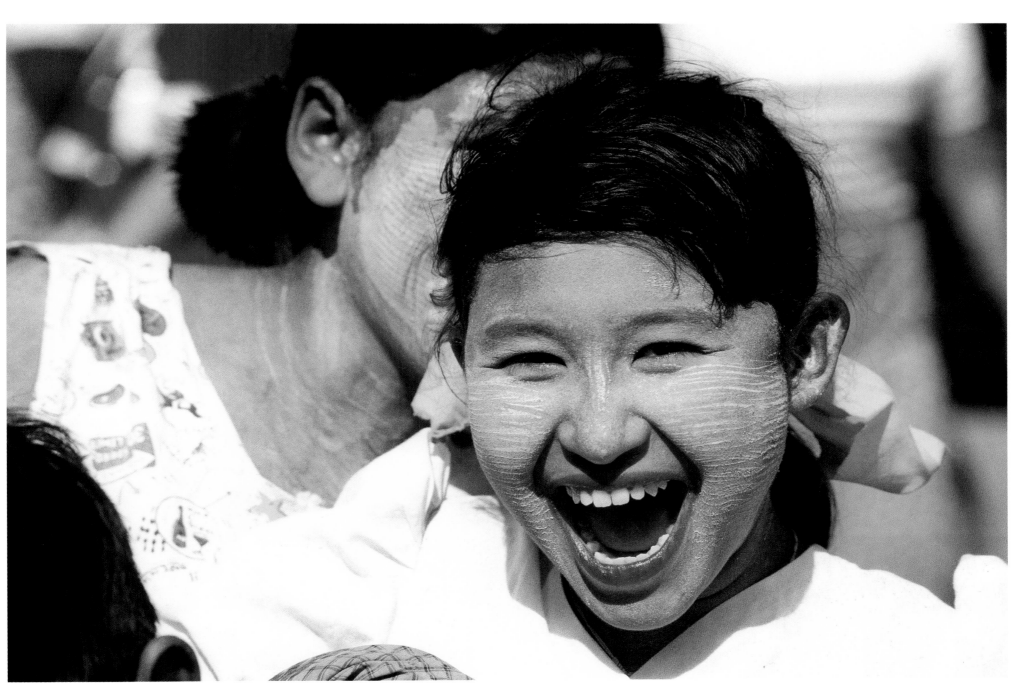

This vibrant Burmese woman has daubed her face with *thanaka*, a popular therapeutic cosmetic made from tree bark, Mandalay, Myanmar (Burma).

photographer Bernard Napthine

number 139

Kids cool off under Seattle's International Fountain, Washington State, USA.
photographer Richard Cummins
number 140

Dashing through the monsoonal downpour that brings relief to the hot streets of Kochi, India.
photographer **Karen Trist**
number 141

A young girl from the scenic village of Sonomarg, which nestles amongst the steep mountainous ridges of the Kashmir Valley, India.
photographer Richard I'Anson
number 142

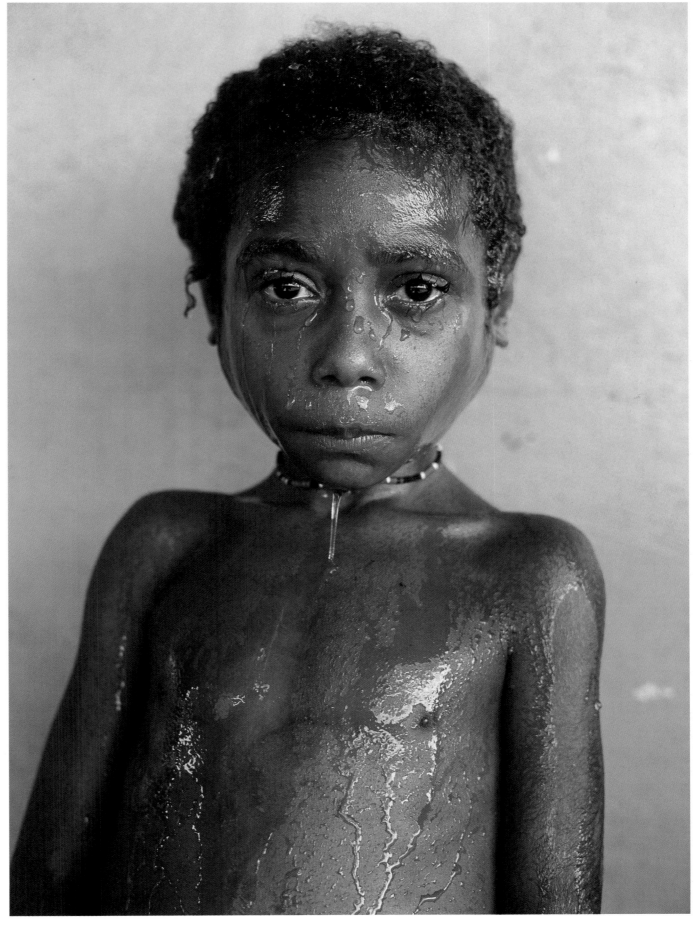

A boy from the Madang province of Papua New Guinea, world-famous for its coral reefs and superb
diving, poses reluctantly, eager to get back to the sea.

photographer Jerry Galea

number 143

A trained cat shows off his prowess for a monk from Nga Phe Kyaung, also known as the 'Jumping Cat'
Monastery, on the shores of Inle Lake, Myanmar (Burma).

photographer Anders Blomqvist

number 144

An elderly man befriends pigeons outside Paris' famous cathedral, Notre Dame, France.
photographer Juliet Coombe
number 145

next page Steam rises from underground vents like a ghostly apparition on a wintry day on New York's 5th Avenue, USA.
photographer Angus Oborn
number 146

A worker keeps an eye on the coke furnace at a steel mill in Talcahuano, Chile.
photographer Eric L Wheater
number 147

Gistock the orang-utan finds sanctuary at the Pondok Tanggui Rehabilitation Centre, buried deep within the tropical rainforest of Tanjung Puting National Park in Kalimantan, Borneo, Indonesia.

photographer Andrew Brownbill

number 148

Travel is more than the seeing of sights; it is a change that goes on, deep and permanent, in the ideas of living.

– Miriam Beard

left Colourfully painted and costumed indigenous tribal groups celebrate the Philippines' Ati-Atihan Festival. This week-long mother of all mardi gras rages from sunrise to sunset and is at its most riotous in Kalibo on Panay Island.

photographer John Pennock

number 149

The construction of the massive Mingun Paya, begun by thousands of slaves in 1790, was never completed. The cracked brick base that stands only a third of the stupa's intended 150-metre height still towers over visiting monks, outside Mandalay, Myanmar (Burma).

photographer Bernard Napthine

number 150

Night draws in over the arid Valle de la Luna (Valley of the Moon) while sunset highlights the Andes, west of San Pedro de Atacama, Chile.

photographer Woods Wheatcroft

number 151

Children of the nomadic Bajau people, known as 'Sea Gypsies', spend their whole lives on boats around the Togean Islands, Indonesia.

photographer Greg Elms

number 152

Young Uyghur boys, Muslims of Turkic descent, play at the Sunday market in Kashgar, China, oblivious to the frantic crowd of pedestrians, bikes and donkey carts arriving to sell their wares at one of Asia's most mind-boggling bazaars.

photographer Richard I'Anson

number 153

These four ancient stones known as the Eightercua Stone Row are thought to be all that remains of a megalithic tomb near Waterville, County Kerry, Ireland.
photographer Richard Cummins
number 154

Sunrise illuminates the granite pillars of the Torres del Paine, a hiker's heaven in Patagonia, southern Chile.
photographer Richard I'Anson
number 155

next page Hitching a buffalo ride to Nyaungshwe on Inle Lake, Myanmar (Burma).
photographer Bernard Napthine
number 156

The steamy window of a bar in Bangkok, Thailand, offers a glimpse of a pool game in action.
photographer Frank Carter
number 157

The hazy atmosphere of the crowded smoking rooms at Gimpo Airport in Seoul, South Korea.
photographer Dennis Johnson
number 158

Treat the earth well. It was not given to you by your parents. It was loaned to you by your children.

- A Kenyan proverb

Wearing an elaborate sun hat, a youngster seeks shelter from the heat in the village of Shoa, Addis Ababa, Ethiopia.

photographer Frances Linzee Gordon

number 160

A rice-paddy worker with the scythe she uses to harvest the rice, near Nha Trang, Vietnam.
photographer Greg Elms
number 161

next page Pink dusk falls across the glacier above Ishinca Valley, Cordillera Blanca, Peru.
photographer Grant Dixon
number 162

Sheltering from the rain in a *bemo* after temple celebrations in Bali, Indonesia.
photographer Gregory Adams
number 163

Australia's iconic Bondi Beach, Sydney, complete with the essential ice-cream van.
photographer Simon Bracken
number 164

Traders working from their boats compare goods at Bangkok's floating market, Thailand.
photographer Greg Elms
number 165

A display of betel leaves at the Bangalore market, India. The leaves are used in the preparation of *paan*
– they are wrapped around a sweet and spicy mixture of mildly narcotic betel nut (a different plant),
lime paste and spices and eaten as a digestive and mouth freshener.

photographer Greg Elms

number 166

A child crouches among the rice harvest in a paddy on Don Khong (Khong Island), Laos.
photographer Bernard Napthine
number 167

Tropical wet season rain can't deter a young swimmer at the local pool in Darwin, Australia.
photographer **Will Salter**
number **168**

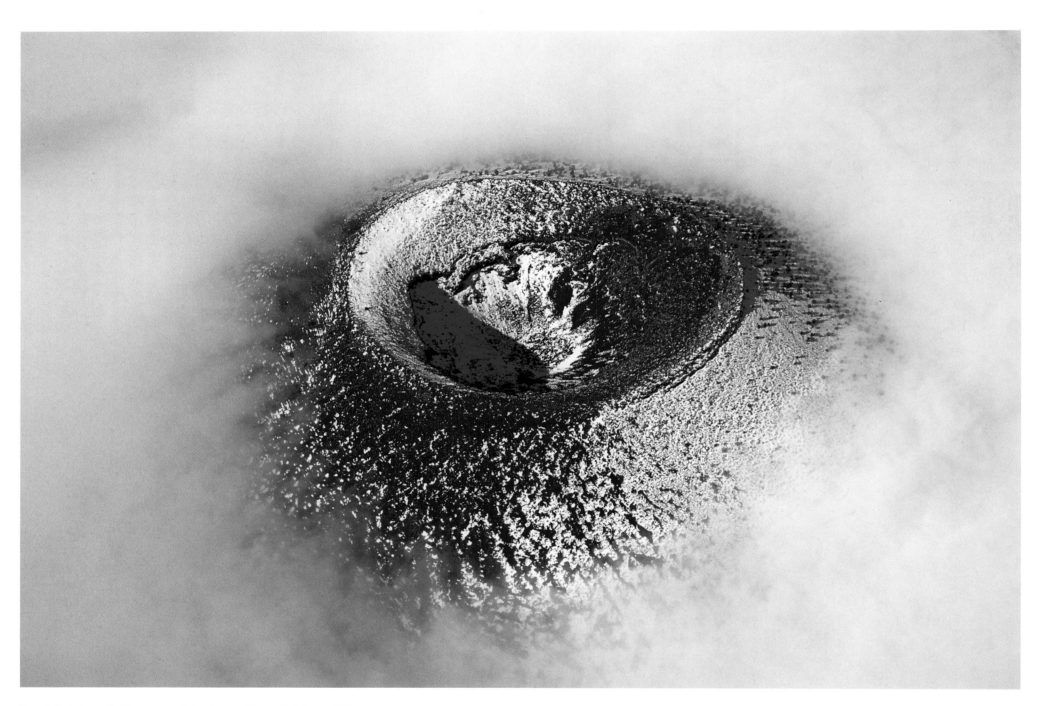

Sunset Crater mantled in snow and clouds, near Flagstaff, Arizona, USA.
photographer **Jim Wark**
number **169**

An icy frozen landscape in Zealand's rural northwest, Denmark.
photographer Martin Lladó
number 170

next page Wildebeest on the move: the furious chaos of up to a million animals in their annual migration across Kenya is a breathtaking sight.
photographer Jason Edwards
number 171

A wild white pelican protects its territory in Lesvos, one of Greece's Northeastern Aegean Islands.
photographer David Tipling
number 172

A lioness shows off her fangs in Kenya's most popular national reserve, the Masai Mara.

photographer **Alex Dissanayake**

number 173

The reflective surfaces of 513 North Michigan Avenue in Chicago, USA.

photographer Richard Cummins

number 174

A reflection of Aladdin Casino in Las Vegas, USA.
photographer Richard Cummins
number 175

A young boy poses with his iguanas, Honduras. Iguanas are common in Honduras, and their passive nature and easy-to-please diet has made them a hit with pet owners.

photographer Jeffrey N Becom

number 176

A tattooed man in a mask stands against a corrugated iron wall – one of the many performances to be found on the streets of the fascinating city of Chiang Mai, northern Thailand.
photographer Bill Wassman
number 177

next page A colourful glimpse of the daily life of novice monks reflected in the windows of Choedhe Gompa in Lo Manthang, Nepal.
photographer Richard l'Anson
number 178

Taking a Sunday walk on the rugged Beara Peninsula, County Cork, Ireland.
photographer Oliver Strewe
number 179

Fresh water can be hard to find in the arid landscape surrounding Van, in southeastern Anatolia, Turkey.
photographer **Izzet Keribar**
number 180

A female green turtle swimming in tropical blue waters off Hawaii, USA.
photographer Simon Foale
number 181

Relaxing in a freshwater pool, or *pemandian*, in Central Java, Indonesia.
photographer Phil Weymouth
number 182

Umbrellas in bloom at the Easter Passion plays in Kalwaria Zebrzydowska, Poland. A blend of religious ceremony and popular theatre re-enacting the last days of Christ's life, the plays have been held in the pilgrimage town since the 17th century – and the wintry weather usually adds a dramatic touch.

photographer Krzysztof Dydynski

number 183

Even in the rain, thousands flock to a purpose-built arena to watch the annual capture of wild horses in Dülmen, Germany. The horses are the only wild breed in Western Europe, and are valued for their small but powerful builds.

photographer David Peevers

number 184

next page Smiles from two young Muslim girls wearing traditional *bui-bui* robes on the offshore island of Lamu, Kenya.

photographer Ariadne Van Zandbergen

number 185

A sapling strives bravely through the winter snow of Oulu, Finland.
photographer David Tipling
number 186

A lone tree is silhouetted against the evening sky in the Masai Mara National Reserve, Kenya.
photographer Christer Fredriksson
number 187

The world is a book and those who do not travel read only a page.

– St Augustine

left Proud troops from Chiang Rai, the northernmost province of Thailand, celebrate the king's birthday
in Bangkok in their traditional dress.
photographer Bill Wassman
number 188

Early morning sun crests the 1000-foot sand dunes on glacial Muztagh-Ata Mountain
(7546 metres) in the Pamir Range, China.
photographer **Keren Su**
number **189**

Rows of rowboats in Tokyo, Japan. The boats are a popular way to view the city's famous cherry blossoms from the moat of the Imperial Palace.

photographer Judy Bellah

number 190

Silhouettes of cactus are reflected in the water at sunset, Saguaro National Park, Arizona, USA.
photographer Richard Cummins
number 191

U Bein's Bridge in Amarapura, Myanmar (Burma), built two centuries ago from teak salvaged from the deserted Inwa Palace, is long and rickety but still used by hundreds of villagers every day.
photographer Bernard Napthine
number 192

next page The Taj Mahal of Agra, India, glows pink in the dawn light. Described as the most extravagant monument ever built for love, the Taj was constructed by Emperor Shah Jahan in memory of his second wife, Mumtaz Mahal, who died in childbirth in 1631.
photographer Dallas Stribley
number 193

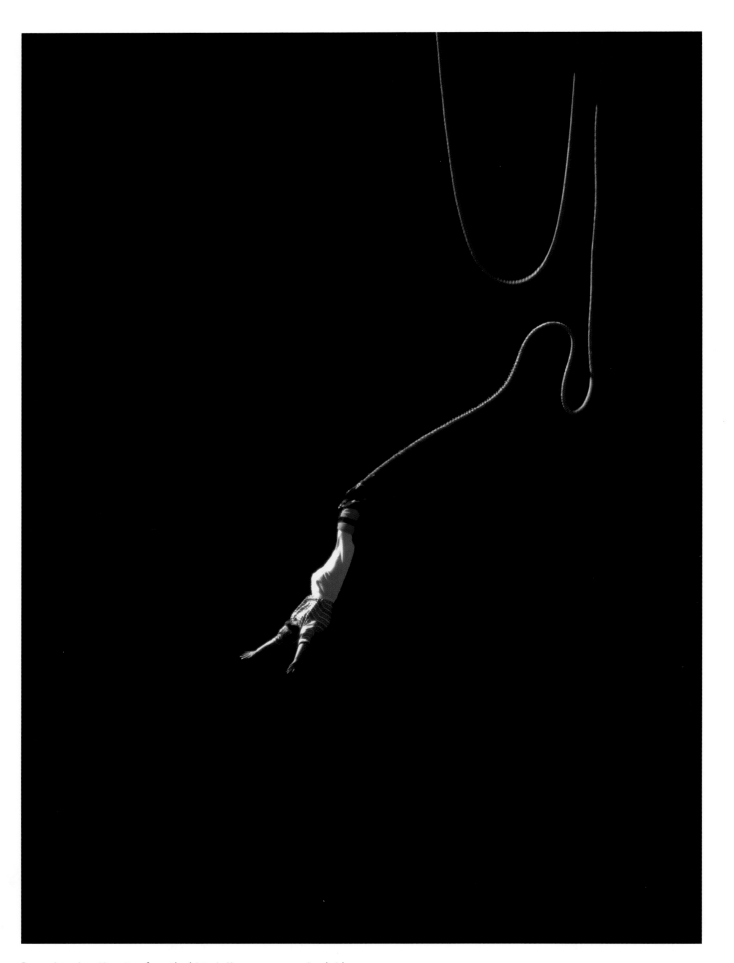

Bungy jumping 43 metres from the historic Kawarau suspension bridge,
the world's first commerical bungy site, near Queenstown, New Zealand.
photographer David Wall
number 194

Passengers on board the *Kapitan Khlebnikov* watch as the ice-cutter
makes its way through the heavy ice of Antarctica's Ross Sea.
photographer Kerry Lorimer

number 195

The turning of the leaves in Machias, Maine, USA.
photographer Jim Wark
number 196

View over the terraced rooftops of the Georgian city of Bath, England.
photographer Jon Davison
number 197

next page A storybook farmhouse on the edge of a field of bright yellow rape, Kullaberg, Sweden.
photographer Anders Blomqvist
number 198

Magnificent alpine views greet walkers on the Cascade Saddle Route in Mount Aspiring National Park, New Zealand, one of the country's premier mountaineering regions.
photographer Gareth McCormack
number 199

Leaping the void in the Wasatch Mountains, Utah, USA.
photographer Cheyenne Rouse
number 200

next page Brightly painted houses create geometric patterns in the old quarter of La Vila Joiosa, a fishing village on the Costa Blanca, Spain. Historically, the houses were painted bright colours to help guide fishing boats into port.
photographer Mark Daffey
number 201

The colours of the sunset reflecting in the surfaces of the Weisman Art Museum, Minneapolis, USA.
photographer Richard Cummins
number 202

Unearthly rock formations in Buckskin Gulch, Utah, USA. Light filters intermittently into this slot canyon, one of the longest and narrowest in the world.

photographer Richard Cummins

number 203

Gridlocked taxis are a familiar sight on Park Avenue, New York City, USA.
photographer Angus Oborn
number 204

Winter darkness descends on the city of Troms, Norway.
photographer Christian Aslund
number 205

next page A small boat glides through a patch of sunlight beneath brewing storm clouds off the southern coast of Thailand.
photographer Greg Elms
number 206

Curiosity is, in great and generous minds, the first passion and the last.
– *Samuel Johnson*

Jellyfish pulsing and wafting in all their ethereal beauty at Monterey Bay Aquarium,
built on the site of what was Monterey's largest sardine cannery, California, USA.
photographer John Elk III
number 208

Parades of richly decorated elephants are a popular highlight of India's many Hindu festivals, including this one in Kochi.

photographer Eddie Gerald

number 209

Our battered suitcases were piled on the sidewalk again; we had longer ways to go. But no matter, the road is life.
- Jack Kerouac

This bridge in Guizhou, China, is a typical example of the unique stone architecture of the Buyi people, which makes use of the abundant building material from the surrounding mountains.

photographer Keren Su
number 211

The weathered Pont y Pen ('Bridge of the Pearl') dates from 1636 and is thought to have been designed by the prolific English architect Inigo Jones. The bridge crosses the River Conwy in North Wales, and leads to the old market town of Llanrwst.

photographer Greg Gawlowski

number 212

What children could resist this muddy slide down a riverbank in Muang Khua, Laos?

photographer Bernard Napthine

number 213

Muddy but content: after a mud bath on the banks of the Rio Grande in Texas, USA.
photographer Oliver Strewe
number 214

A farmer cleans a paddy field in the dawn light, Bali, Indonesia.
photographer Gregory Adams
number 215

Trees peep out of a carpet of fog at Goulais Point on Lake Superior, Ontario, Canada.

photographer **Jim Wark**

number 216

An Arizona couple of the Navajo tribe proudly display their traditional silver-and-turquoise jewellery, USA.

photographer Dallas Stribley

number 217

Highway collectors for charity enjoy an ice-cream break on the road near Guadalajara, Mexico.
photographer Greg Elms
number 218

next page Shrouded in cloud, the spectacular active volcanic peak of Mount Ngauruhoe (2287 metres)
overlooks Tongariro National Park, World Heritage area and New Zealand's oldest national park.
photographer Dennis Johnson
number 219

A Brahmin girl in Helambhu, Nepal, prepares for her wedding ceremony: a bridal procession to the groom's house, followed by a feast of 84 traditional dishes which will symbolise the couple's union.
photographer Bill Wassman
number 220

A local fisherman mends his nets in preparation for another day's fishing on the reefs around Ko Si Chang, a small rocky island off the eastern coast of Thailand.

photographer Bill Wassman

number 221

Visitors' wooden sandals neatly lined up in front of Daitoku-ji, a tranquil
Zen temple and garden complex founded in 1319 in Kyoto, Japan.

photographer Frank Carter

number 222

Thongs and sandals are discarded as dancers practise for a temple festival in the very traditional village of Timbrah, Bali, Indonesia.
photographer Gregory Adams
number 223

Djenné's extraordinary Grande Mosquée, in Mali, is a classic example of Sahel-style mud architecture, and is the largest mud-brick building in the world.
photographer David Else
number 224

The old walls of Essaouira on Morocco's Atlantic coast are weathered by the ever-present wind and sand.

photographer Olivier Cirendini

number 225

Street wallpaper on Rue Saint Denis in Montreal, Canada.
photographer Alain Evrard
number 226

A fortune-teller displays his palmistry readings on Gandhi Irwin Road, Chennai, India.
photographer Greg Elms
number 227

next page A child of the Moken people perches on one of Ko Lipe's beaches. Also known as 'Sea Gypsies', the Moken live on houseboats and in semi-permanent stilt villages off Thailand's Andaman coast, subsisting largely on fish from the surrounding coral reefs.
photographer Paul Beinssen
number 228

Drying the essentials in an inner-city back yard, Melbourne, Australia.
photographer David Hannah
number 229

Bright towels hung neatly to dry outside a house on the Kamogawa riverside in Kyoto, Japan.
photographer Frank Carter
number 230

The ceremonial changing of the guard in front of the Tomb of the Unknown Soldier at Athens' parliament building, Greece.

photographer Diana Mayfield

number 231

The guards at Athens' parliament building are known as *evzones* as they are traditionally recruited from the Macedonian village of Evzoni. Their tunics and pom-pom shoes derive from the attire worn by the *klephts* (mountain fighters) in the Greek War of Independence.

photographer Diana Mayfield

number 232

The 'Leopard Ladies' are a mother and daughter team who stroll the streets welcoming festival-goers to Cannes, France. For many, these local personalities are an essential part of the city's famous film festival.

photographer Dan Herrick

number 233

Of the astounding density of wildlife in the Masai Mara National Reserve, Kenya, leopards are among the hardest animals to spot, but lions, elephants, buffaloes, zebras, hippos, antelopes and myriad other species are commonly seen, often in one place at one time.

photographer Alex Dissanayake

number 234

A jaunty-looking mannequin models some of the goods available at a clothing store in Shimla, India.
photographer Greg Elms
number 235

Sporting sunglasses against the fierce glare of the Egyptian sun at Cairo's main bus stop.
photographer Phil Weymouth
number 236

Tourists enjoy the superb snorkelling off Rábida (Jervis) Island, one of Ecuador's Galápagos Islands which is known for its unusual beaches with their dark red volcanic sand.

photographer Richard I'Anson

number 237

Southern fur seals frolic at Seal Rocks on Phillip Island, a popular holiday resort in Victoria, Australia.
photographer **Simon Foale**
number **238**

The black-faced sheep of Normandy graze before the Benedictine abbey on the summit of Mont St-Michel, France.

photographer Olivier Cirendini

number 239

A farmer shoots quail amid the wheat stubble, backed by the huge empty horizon of Victoria's Mallee region, Australia.

photographer John Hay

number 240

A local man strikes a playful pose for the camera in Ubud, the cultural centre of Bali, Indonesia.
photographer Gregory Adams
number 241

A well-groomed competitor waits patiently for judging to begin at the Royal Melbourne Agricultural Show, Australia, where the country comes to town for livestock and craft displays, rodeos and showjumping.
photographer Phil Weymouth
number 242

LONELY PLANET: SEE IT FOR YOURSELF
September 2003
Reprinted 2004

Publisher: Roz Hopkins
Art Director: Jane Pennells
Photographic Adviser: Richard I'Anson
Project Manager: Bridget Blair
Design Manager: Karina Dea
Designers: Gerilyn Attebery, Wendy Wright, Rodney Zandbergs, Brendan Dempsey
Editors: Janet Austin, Meaghan Amor
Pre-press Production: Ryan Evans
Print Production: Graham Imeson

Thanks to: Lou Byrnes, Peter D'Onghia, Jain Lemos, Katrina Webb

Published by
Lonely Planet Publications Pty Ltd ABN 36 005 607 983
90 Maribyrnong St, Footscray, Victoria 3011, Australia

www.lonelyplanet.com
AOL keyword: lp

Printed by the Bookmaker International Ltd
Printed in China

Photographs
The images in this book are available for licensing from Lonely Planet Images.
www.lonelyplanetimages.com

ISBN 1 74059 874 1

text © Lonely Planet Publications Pty Ltd 2003
photographs © photographers as indicated 2003

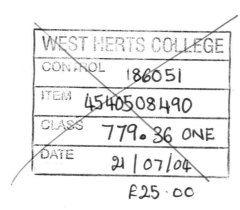

Lonely Planet Offices

Australia
90 Maribyrnong St, Footscray, Victoria, 3011
tel: 03 8379 8000
fax: 03 8379 8111
email: talk2us@lonelyplanet.com.au

USA
150 Linden St, Oakland, CA 94607
tel: 510 893 8555 TOLL FREE: 800 275 8555
fax: 510 893 8572
email: info@lonelyplanet.com

UK
72-82 Rosebery Ave
London EC1R 4RW
tel: 020 7841 9000
fax: 020 7841 9001
email: go@lonelyplanet.co.uk

France
1 rue du Dahomey, 75011 Paris
tel: 01 55 25 33 00
fax: 01 55 25 33 01
email: bip@lonelyplanet.fr